Broadway Christian
My Life is in Your Hands
Troccoli, Kathy

P9-DDB-711

0000 4410

MY LIFE IS IN YOUR HANDS

MY LIFE IS IN YOUR HANDS

K A T H Y   T R O C C O L I

DEVOTIONS TO HELP YOU FALL MORE DEEPLY IN LOVE WITH JESUS

ZondervanPublishingHouse

Grand Rapids, Michigan

A Division of HarperCollins*Publishers*

My Life Is in Your Hands
Copyright © 1997 by Kathy Troccoli

Requests for information should be addressed to:

ZondervanPublishingHouse
Grand Rapids, Michigan 49530

Library of Congress Cataloging-in-Publication Data

Troccoli, Kathy.
    My life is in Your hands : devotions to help you fall more deeply in
love with Jesus / Kathy Troccoli.
        p.   cm.
        ISBN: 0-310-21061-5 (hardcover)
    1. Meditations. I. Title.
BV4832.2.T765   1997
242—dc21   97-26778
                                                                            CIP

This edition is printed on acid-free paper and meets the American
National Standards Institute Z39.48 standard.

Interior design by Sue Vandenberg Koppenol

Printed in the United States of America

---

97 98 99 00 01 02 03 04 /❖ DC/ 10 9 8 7 6 5 4 3 2 1

For Allyson Rice Baker
because certain friendships only
come along once in a lifetime.

CONTENTS

ACKNOWLEDGMENTS

Ann Spangler, for looking past the singer to find the author.

Linda Montero, for keen eyes, endless hours, and a patient heart. Life has been easier.

Dorothy Ophals, for consistently demonstrating a servant's heart.

Cindy Dupree, for supporting me through yet another adventure.

Ellie Lofaro, for convincing me that I didn't have to be smart to write a book.

MY LIFE IS IN YOUR HANDS

Life can be so good
Life can be so hard
Never knowing what each day
Will bring to where you are.

Sometimes I forget
Sometimes I can't see
That whatever comes my way
You'll be with me.

My life is in your hands
My heart is in your keeping
I'm never without hope
Not when my future is with you
My life is in your hands
And though I may not see clearly
I will lift my voice and sing
'Cause your love does amazing things
Lord, I know
My life is in your hands.

Nothing is for sure
Nothing is for keeps
All I know is that your love
Will live eternally.

So I will find my rest
And I will find my peace

Knowing that
You'll meet my every need.

When I'm at my weakest
Oh, You carry me
Then I become my strongest
Lord, in your hands.

My life is in your hands
And though I may not see clearly
I will lift my voice and sing
'Cause your love does amazing things
Lord, I know
My life is in your hands
I trust you, Lord
My life is in your hands.

Kathy Troccoli

DO YOU KNOW HOW MUCH I LOVE YOU?

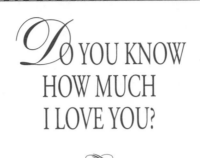

And I pray that you, being rooted and established in love, may have power, together with all the saints, to grasp how wide and long and high and deep is the love of Christ, and to know this love that surpasses knowledge—that you may be filled to the measure of all the fullness of God.

Ephesians 3:17-19

When my niece Gina was very little we would engage in that familiar exchange you have with children you're crazy about. I asked her one day, "Do you know how much I love you?"

She looked at me with eager and excited expectation.

"All the way to the sky," I said.

She climbed into my lap. "Well, I love you all the way to the ocean," she said.

"Oh yeah?" I squeezed her tight and tickled her gently. "Well, I love you all the way to heaven."

"Well, I love you . . ." she began, then, "I love . . . I love you . . ." She contemplated her answer most intensely. Finally, taking a deep breath, she said, "I love you all the way to K-Mart in the toy department."

The two of us laughed and laughed. Gina thought she had given me the biggest and best possible answer.

We humans want desperately to express the love we feel. Passionately, we give it a color, a taste, a word, an action that will assure the other person we've given all we've got.

But we are limited. Our time, our emotions, our expressions can only reach so far and so deep. After my precious encounter with Gina I was reminded of the Lord's love. What a lavish God we serve. His expressions of love and commitment to us are limitless. He keeps every promise he makes. His giving is never-ending—an eternal fountain, flowing forever. His life pours into us as we open ourselves to him. His love is unconditional. Faithful. "For I am convinced that neither death nor life, neither angels nor demons, neither the present nor the future, nor any powers, neither height nor depth, nor anything else in all creation, will be able to separate us from the love of God that is in Christ Jesus our Lord" (Romans 8:38–39).

Know how much he loves you this day. Don't mistake your ability to love or understand with his ability to love and understand. I suppose if you told Jesus, "I love you all the way to . . ." he would answer back that he loved you all the way to the cross—and that he'll continue to love you throughout eternity. It takes your breath away, and you can only respond with a heart of thankfulness.

I'm so thankful—
    for you, Lord,
  and for all that you are—
I praise you
  and thank you once again
      for all you've done for me,
    and for all the blessings you've
      rained down on me.

∞

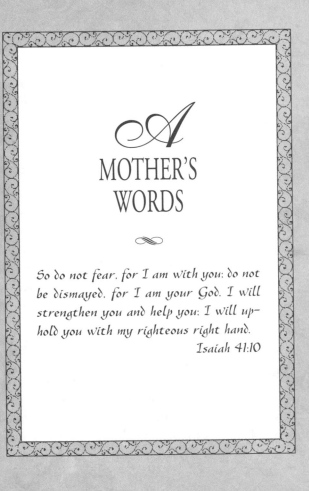

A
MOTHER'S
WORDS

∞

So do not fear, for I am with you; do not be dismayed, for I am your God. I will strengthen you and help you; I will uphold you with my righteous right hand.

Isaiah 41:10

When I was growing up, my mother would repeat certain favorite phrases. Friends and I still laugh about some of them. My sister and I regularly remind each other of those bold "words of wisdom" she would often quote to us. In the last couple of years since her death, remembering these phrases and how she would speak them, brings me comfort.

Whenever we forgot to turn off the lights my mother would say loudly, "What do you think, Edison is your father?" Or the infamous statement, "Money doesn't grow on trees." Or how about her answer to roughhousing: "Well, it's all fun and games until someone gets hurt." Whenever I hear someone say, "I'm thirsty," I hear my mother's voice and see the little smirk on her face as she says, "Well, I'm Friday." Every one of these familiar sayings brings a smile to my face. I'm sure we could all write a book on "mother quotes and quips." Nobody said it quite like Mom.

My mother died of cancer. She showed amazing courage throughout her illness and handled the dying process with dignity and humility. She was prodded, poked, operated on, and carted back and forth to hospitals, but she never once complained, only confessed that she was "getting tired." Before my eyes she lived out the truth of another of her favorite phrases: "God will give you strength when you need it."

Of all the words my mother spoke, I think that statement has meant the most. When I was in the middle of the most difficult times of my life—the struggles, the tears, the dark days—she would offer those tender words. Now, as I look back and see that God really was with me, giving me grace to bear the unbearable, I realize that my mother was right. More than that, I know she spoke the heart of God. And so, besides all Mom's funny phrases, she also gave me some serious gems that I cherish and still cling to.

There is no situation in this life that he will not miraculously lead us through—giving us a strength and peace that we know is beyond anything we could conjure up. Lean on him. Abandon yourself to his grace. God will give you strength when you need it.

Winds,
   heavy rain,
      gushing waters.
In the midst
   of any storm
You
   are my anchor....
I shall not be moved....

WHOSE FACE IS IT?

❧

Do not be proud, but be willing to associate with people of low position. Do not be conceited.

Romans 12:16

friend and I were engrossed in conversation on our way somewhere on a hot California afternoon. She happens to own a beautiful BMW, complete with all the extras and an amazing sound system. As we stopped at a corner, over the music and over the talk, I heard a voice outside my window. A lady, obviously weathered from the streets, stood a few feet away from our car. Dirty. Hungry. They all look the same, laying on the sidewalk, park bench, or church steps. We've become accustomed to this familiar sight. Some of us turn away in disgust and some in sympathy. I try to challenge myself to turn in the way that Jesus would. Are these the faces of "soulless" people, or the faces of Christ? How can we sum up their situation and background in just a matter of seconds as we drive by?

Jesus spoke to this issue directly in Matthew 25:42–45: "'For I was hungry and you gave me nothing to eat, I was thirsty and you gave me nothing to drink, I was a stranger and you did not invite me in, I needed clothes and you did not clothe me, I was sick and in prison and you did not look after me.' They also will answer, 'Lord, when did we see you hungry or thirsty or a stranger or needing clothes or sick or in prison, and did not help you?' He will reply, 'I tell you the truth, whatever you did not do for one of the least of these, you did not do for me.'"

We smile at the beautiful little girl walking by us at the mall, we greet the Fed Ex man with courtesy, we ask for autographs at concerts, we sometimes stop for the motorist stranded on the side of the road, we greet visitors at our churches—the list goes on and on. The Bible acknowledges our ease at loving the lovely and our resistance to loving the unlovely. I believe that Christ is disguised in men today just as he was after he rose from the dead.

"How about a turkey sandwich and some hot coffee?" I asked the woman on the corner.

She said with an expressionless face, "Yeah, that would be great."

It was a small contribution to my Jesus who is hungry and thirsty in people all over the world. May we be aware of his presence in humanity. May we be aware of his need in the needs of others. May we offer his love outside of the boundaries of our own love. May we never let our hearts become so numb and so blind that we cannot see the face of Jesus in the people we meet in the everyday of our lives.

Eyes
   speak
      so easily:
   the giving,
      reaching-to-touch,
         love-filled words
      our mouths
         so desperately
            try to say.
   Let
      the eyes
         you've
            created for me
      master
         the words,
   "Jesus loves you."

HE WILL PROTECT YOU

❧

Your statutes are my delight; they are my counselors.... preserve my life according to your word.

Psalm 119:24-25

Spanish woman came up to me after one of my concerts. She was bubbly and colorful and full of life. I could tell immediately that she had a true love for God and a childlike excitement about knowing him. We talked and shared for awhile and then she said she wanted to show me something special.

She began to tell me about her father, who loved Jesus and had fought in World War II. He found himself in a fierce battle one day, in which gunfire exploded and grenades blew up all around him. He survived, she said, because a miracle had happened. She then pulled a tiny Bible from her purse. She told me he had always carried it in his chest pocket, right next to his heart. I took it in my hands; a hole was blown through each and every page all the way to the back cover. I marveled at this act of God.

The word of the Lord. By this man's heart. It protected him. In the same way, he wants to protect you and me every day of our lives. How often do we fail in letting

God's Word protect our hearts? We too often lean into the circumstance or the emotion rather than God's truth about us. I can sometimes surrender to battles without even giving a thought to the words, ". . . in all these things we are more than conquerors through him who loved us" (Romans 8:37). Guilt hangs over me like a dark cloud before I acknowledge that, ". . . there is now no condemnation for those who are in Christ Jesus" (Romans 8:1). In the eighth chapter of Romans alone I can win many wars that rage in and around my soul. In walking through tragic, trying situations, "consider that our present sufferings are not worth comparing with the glory that will be revealed in us" (Romans 8:18). When I can hardly look up toward heaven and can barely mutter a prayer, "In the same way, the Spirit helps us in our weakness. We do not know what we ought to pray for, but the Spirit himself intercedes for us with groans that words cannot express" (Romans 8:26). When I have trouble understanding hardship, "We know that in all things God works for the good of those who love him, who have been called according to his purpose" (Romans 8:28). When I feel misunderstood, slandered, and put up against the wall, "If God is for us, who can be against us?" (Romans 8:31).

I could go on and on. And the above is just one chapter from the whole of Scripture. God's Word is eternal, unchanging, faithful, true. It is not feelings, it is the Word of God. It is not circumstances, it is the Word of God. It is not our words that matter, but his. Keep them by your heart. They will surely protect you.

Lord,
  teach me
    to give my very all
  to this life
    that you've given me,
      but
    to always remember
      to save my heart
        for you.

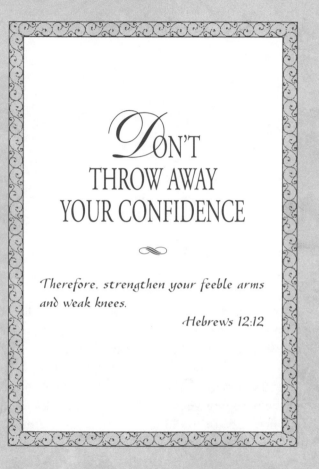

DON'T THROW AWAY YOUR CONFIDENCE

∾

Therefore, strengthen your feeble arms and weak knees.

Hebrews 12:12

This has always been one of my favorite verses. At those times when I feel like I can't even get out of bed and face another day, it encourages me.

Our capacity to feel, to think, and to experience is so great—to taste the sweetness of joy that life can bring, to bask in the peace of God, to worship on the mountaintops, to ride high on loving and being loved. All of these are wonderful and precious gifts, and I'm so thankful for them as I journey through this earthly life.

But oh, the downfall when we rely on these experiences as the truth or believe in them as the absolute. For when the sweetness goes sour, the storm comes raging in, the dryness hits, or the loneliness prevails, we must continually remember that God's truth never changes. My feelings do, my circumstances do, but his truth never does. I *must* push beyond it all and make a choice. Christianity. The Sovereign hand of God in my life—but my choice; to have faith, to go on, to *lift* my drooping hands, to *strengthen* my weak knees, and *make* a straight path for my feet. All my choice. All things that the Lord has told me to do so that he may come in and work on my behalf. As I yield he can and he will act. Then yes, what is lame can be healed: hopelessness, doubt, fear, anger, bitterness, insecurity.

Through prayer, however feeble the utterance, through standing on his Word—or should I say falling on his Word if we're too weak—God will *come*.

We must choose him. As the Bible tells us in Hebrews 10:35–36, "Do not throw away your confidence; it will be richly rewarded. You need to persevere so that when you have done the will of God, you will receive what he has promised."

Father,
    help me
        to throw out
    all
        the dirty
            old
        dusty memorabilia
            in
        every corner
            of my heart.
I know,
    it's only
        taking up space
    in the places where
        you want to
            place your love.
You're welcome
        to go through everything—
    my most treasured possessions—
if it will give you
    more room
        to live.

HEROES

∞

And he will be called Wonderful Coun-
selor, Mighty God, Everlasting Father,
Prince of Peace.

Isaiah 9:6

I was on one of my many visits to Frank and Ellie's house. Knowing them has taught me a lot and brought me much comfort. As I've watched their marriage and their interaction with their three children, as I've accepted their invitation to make their home my home away from home, I have become a better person. They are an inspiration to me to someday be a good wife and mother, to create an environment for my own future family that promotes peace and love and wholeness.

I have enjoyed numerous lazy mornings at the Lofaro home, where we sleep in, devour Frank's generous buffet breakfast heaped with bagels, pastries, and fruit, and hang out in pajamas until noon has come and gone. I would never have imagined myself in my thirties spending so much time watching Barney, Davey and Goliath, and all sorts of other animated musicals—and enjoying it.

One particular morning, after everyone but Ellie and I had left the breakfast table, little Jordan climbed into his mother's arms. We continued talking, but I watched this small boy's face as he looked at his mother. He seemed so content, so safe, so cared for. Detouring from our conversation for a moment, I asked Jordan what he loved about her. His five-year-old heart quickly responded, "She's my friend." He thought a little more, then, "She's my hero." Finally, with a deep sigh, he said, "She's my everything."

Ellie hugged and kissed him, and I was reminded of the many, many times I have felt content and safe in the arms of Jesus, trusting my life, my concerns, and my hopes into his care.

He longs to hold you, to care for you. He longs to meet your needs and for you to put your trust in him. He is a faithful God with arms that will never let you go. Ask me why I love him and you'll receive the same response that I received from Jordan. He's my friend. He's my hero. He's my everything.

A childlike faith,
where I trust
and
simply believe
I want that kind of heart.

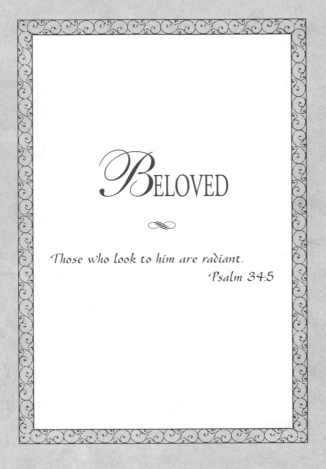

BELOVED

❦

Those who look to him are radiant.

Psalm 34:5

What an incredible paradox I live in. To understand who I am without God and what I'm capable of without Jesus is so sobering. I'm easily subject to passions, lusts, lies, idols, sin, and death. At the same time, I know who I am in Jesus: a conqueror, a child of God, a sinner saved by grace, a receiver of the gift of heaven.

I move in greater strength, growth, maturity, and grace when I keep this balancing truth in my heart and mind: "Wretched woman that I am, but beautiful bride of Christ."

Internal voices tell me I look horrible, fat, and unattractive, and that I always will. When I listen to these blows to my self-esteem, I let them crush my ability to see the truth of who God says I am, all he says I will become, all he desires for me, and all that he promised me. I am beautiful, lovely, and radiant *only* when I look to him, *only* when I listen to his words, and what he says about me. When, through obedience, I allow his character to become my character, he fills and covers all the holes of insecurity I've dug for myself.

Jesus is my beauty. He is my loveliness, my confidence. He is the charisma, the attractiveness that is right and true—that breeds life not death. That points to good and not evil. Jesus. The perfume the world, our family, and our friends will take notice of. What is she wearing? Jesus. The answer must be Jesus.

Mary Magdalene understood the meaning of "wretched woman that I am, but beautiful bride of Christ." She never forgot where she came from, what she was saved from, what she was capable of, and where she'd be without God. But Mary became God's woman, his person, his precious and beautiful bride. Jesus loved her, saved her, believed for her when she didn't even know there was another way, another life, a new and holy journey.

We are all Marys in some sort of way. Wretched women but beautiful brides. Sinners but saved. Broken but beloved. All because he lives in us. Walk confidently this day, knowing that Jesus will shine through you as you look to him.

"Mary
   took about a pint
      of pure nard,
         an expensive perfume;
she poured it
   on Jesus' feet
      and wiped
         his feet with her hair.
And the house
   was filled
      with the fragrance
         of the perfume."
Jesus,
   teach me to kneel
      at your feet,
   to talk with you,
      watch you,
         hear you,
            worship you,
   so that
      my prayers and praise
         are like that costly ointment
   and all of heaven
      filled with the fragrance
         of our time together.

                              John 12:3

THE EVER-SHINING LIGHT

Let us walk in the light of the LORD.

Isaiah 2:5

*M*y bus driver's name on this particular spring tour was "Shooter." He was kindhearted, upbeat, and very unassuming. He always greeted me with a smile and, most importantly, he delivered me safely to my destinations.

Shooter's kindness exhibited itself in many small, yet profound, ways. I'll never forget the day I had a bad virus and could hardly lift my pounding head. I had a fever and chills, and my chest was so congested, I coughed every two minutes. I wanted to be in my own bed so badly. Hot tea was available in the hotel lobby, but just putting on my clothes was a chore. The thought of getting there exhausted me. But I mustered up the energy and walked out my door. Shooter immediately saw me, ran over, and asked how I was feeling. Then he bent down to tie my untied shoelaces. His gesture was so very kind.

I remember another day on the road. In dire need of toiletries, I was waiting in the lobby for a cab to take me to the nearest drug store. Shooter also happened to be there, so we chatted for awhile.

Out of the blue, he said to me, "Kathy, you get up in the morning with a good attitude. You smile. You're kind. I like that."

Most of our city-to-city traveling is done during the night hours, at which time we're asleep in our bunks for five, six, ten, or more hours. This is the only way we can tour day after day.

I was humbled at his words. *Nowhere near every morning,* I thought. But I was thankful for his observation.

"Well, Shooter," I said, "none of this matters if I don't live or strive to live what I sing about. I fall awfully short, but I'm glad you see something good."

"Well, this is how I look at it," he said. "The sun comes up every morning, and I'm grateful for another day to be alive. And you know what? If the sun never came up, we could all use a flashlight."

Shooter's words touched me deeply that day. I am a believer in Jesus and his promises: If the sun doesn't shine I do indeed have a flashlight—his word a lamp unto my feet guiding my every step; his eyes seeing for me when I am too blind to see; his fire setting my heart ablaze so that I can see my sin and allow his love to consume it. The sweet glow of his presence shines into my darkness. His touch is upon my pain. His mercy covers me. And as I have received, I can give; I can hold out my flashlight, enabling others to see and be comforted when the sun is not shining and the days are like nights.

We must not sit in the dark. We must remember what we have in him. His light and his love are ever shining.

Even
  in the
    uttermost depths
  of
    the darkness,
I see
  before me
    your light
      of hope,
your light
  of faith,
    and your light
      of love burning
        deep within me,
giving
  me
    an unspeakable,
      peaceful,
        assurance,
knowing
  you will perform
  what
    you
    have spoken.

≫

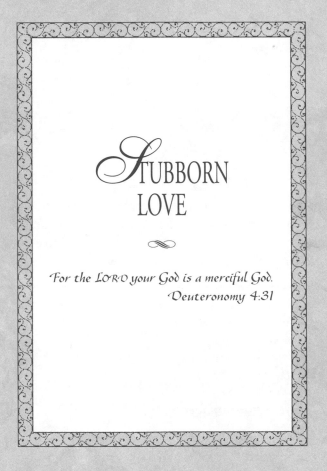

STUBBORN LOVE

❧

For the LORD your God is a merciful God.
Deuteronomy 4:31

I recorded a song in the early eighties that I still listen to from time to time. Thousands of songs have been written about the love of God, but this one expresses my feelings about it in a way that few have.

> *It's your stubborn love*
> *   that never lets go of me*
> *I don't understand*
> *   how you can stay*
> *Perfect love embracing*
> *   the worst in me*
> *How I long for*
> *   your stubborn love.*

Perfect love embracing the worst in me. It is so hard to comprehend that kind of a love. I'm sure all of us have at times related to the Lord as if he loves like we do—imperfectly; this would include guilt trips, resentment, bitterness, and punishment. I've wasted much time in my relationship with him because I have felt I couldn't approach him. I have kept my distance from the Lord until *I* felt like I could get back into right relationship with him or return to his good graces.

But Jesus loves us with an absolute pure love. When I'm finally still, he reveals himself to me, and gives me all I need for righteousness, and a glorious relationship with him. One particular story in scripture has shown me this side of the Lord's heart. I read it often to remind me of the truth.

Peter was a zealous, outspoken apostle. A tenacious man, he spoke with severe conviction. On the night of Jesus' arrest, he told his disciples they would fall away from him. Peter immediately began to argue with Jesus; if all fell away, he never would. Jesus then said that on that very night, before the rooster crowed, Peter would deny him three times. Peter declared, "Even if I have to die with you, I will never disown you" (Matthew 26:35). Yes, it was just like Peter to say that—and yes, he did deny him. At three different times, Peter was asked about his association with Jesus, and three times he vehemently denied it.

> Immediately a rooster crowed. Then Peter remembered the word Jesus had spoken: "Before the rooster crows you will disown me three times." And he went outside and wept bitterly. (Matthew 26:74–75)

It humbles me to think about how alike Peter and I are—the sin, the denial, the guilt—sometimes a numbness, sometimes a lack of guilt that in itself causes me guilt. I wrestle and grieve and find a big chasm between me and God. When will I learn that his disposition never changes? When will I learn that in throwing myself at his mercy—mercy will always embrace me?

After Jesus was buried, Mary Magdalene and Mary the mother of James went to the tomb to anoint his body, but when they arrived, they saw that the stone had been rolled away from the entrance. As they entered the tomb, they were alarmed to see a young man in a white robe.

> "Don't be alarmed," he said. "You are looking for Jesus the Nazarene, who was crucified. He has risen! He is not here. See the place where they laid him. But go, tell his disciples and Peter, 'He is going ahead of you into Galilee. There you will see him, just as he told you.'" (Mark 16:6–7)

Go tell his disciples *and* Peter. Remarkable. What a personal touch from God. Can you imagine what Peter felt like when he heard this? Smothered by mercy. Embraced by the hands that created the world. Pierced by a love that reaches above and beyond anything he'd ever known.

Like this apostle, you too are remembered by Jesus. Never forsaken. Mercy is waiting to gather you into its arms and remind you of the stubborn love of God.

Thank you, Lord,
  that you always forgive,
    that you're always ready
      to receive,
    and that you love me
      like no other.

∞

REAL LIFE

≈

My message and my preaching were not
with wise and persuasive words, but with
a demonstration of the Spirit's power, so
that your faith might not rest on men's
wisdom, but on God's power.

1 Corinthians 2:4-5

More and more these days I am hearing derogatory remarks aimed towards Christians:

"They are all a bunch of hypocrites."

"Can you believe he told me I'm going to hell?"

"All she does is preach at me."

"They don't respect what I believe—they just want me to accept what they believe."

And on and on. I am often amazed at how I see my brothers and sisters representing the gospel, representing Jesus to a world so in need of him. As I talk about Christianity to people, it's hard for me to refute some of the criticisms. I'm challenged and often find that I have to climb over many stereotypes the world has placed upon believers. I do know that, ultimately, when everyone stands before God, the fact that "the church is hypocritical" will not be sufficient reason for not believing in Christ as Savior. I can see the Lord saying something like, "What is that to you? I've asked *you* to follow me." I've often said that if we compare ourselves to the worst in other people, we may come out looking pretty good, but if we compare ourselves to Jesus, we will certainly hang our heads low.

We must do away with evangelistic rules based on our own agendas and personal experiences. We must strive to hear the Lord and be the Lord in our everyday lives—and he may look different and sound different according to the needs of those around us. God wants to give his life to people. L-I-F-E. We can use these letters to remind us of how to do just that:

L—Be a good listener. I have to work hard on this one. Most of us like to talk about ourselves. We must be quiet long enough to truly hear the concerns and the heart of another. We must be patient to let others speak, so that when they leave our presence, they know we have sincerely heard them.

I—Be inquisitive. How can we meet a need when we don't know what the need is? I'm not talking about being nosy, but a kind of inquisitiveness that is full of kindness and is attentive, even enthusiastic—a kind of genuine interest that allows someone to talk about a job, family, or personal background without intimidation. This kind of care will cause others to feel safe with you.

F—Be an advocate of freedom. We must allow others to be who they truly are and not force them to think, be, or act a certain way before they even know Christ or have any motivation to do so. His kindness is what will lead them to repentance. Jesus accepts us where we are. The "gods" in our lives are usually torn down and crushed *after* we know what they actually are. Still, even after a person sincerely desires to please God and *knows* what pleases him—even then—the struggle can be great. Mercy. We must have mercy.

E—Be an example. Simple and to the point—live what you believe. Represent Jesus in your person. Cause the world to want what you have. What an awesome calling. Others will only desire the Jesus in you if he is revealed through your life.

Let the world hear him through your voice, see him in your eyes, touch him through your touch, and find him in the treasures of your heart. The apostle Paul said, "You yourselves are our letter, written on our hearts, known and read by everybody" (2 Corinthians 3:2). May we be a book others can't put down until they, too, have put their life and soul into the hands of God.

I celebrate
　　your birth in me
　　　　all those years ago.
　　　　A toast
Instead of a glass,
　　I lift my heart high
　　　　and touch it
　　　　　　to yours.
Jesus,
　　here's to life in you.

∞

MOMMY, CAN SHE BE OURS?

※

He said to them. "Let the little children come to me. and do not hinder them. for the kingdom of God belongs to such as these."

Mark 10:14

Often after concerts I stay and greet the people who come. It is important that I have that kind of exchange at the end of the night. Many memories are made as I sit for hours at a time and look into the faces of everyone willing to wait. It is a humbling experience for me—such a tender gift from God—to have those quality moments with people, however short. Way beyond the pictures and autographs—it's the stories, the tears, the hugs, the prayers, the pages and chapters from the books of life—that for all of us are somehow strangely connected and amazingly the same. I'm sure people have no idea how much I'm encouraged and blessed by these times; I learn so much from their comments and interactions, and I take home eternal truths.

One particular night as I signed autographs, a woman came up to me with a sweet, blond, curly-haired little girl by her side. "Kathy," she said, "during your concert all my daughter kept saying was 'Mommy, can she be

58

ours?'" This touched me deeply, and I reached over and hugged the child. Then, a few moments later, this little girl ran up to me in tears. Her mother followed, saying that her daughter didn't want to leave—she wanted me to come home with them. Deeply warmed, I went to sleep that night with this child and her tears on my heart.

I know that music and concerts and popularity can draw people in, but somehow I want to believe that this child had seen Jesus—even a glimpse of him—in me. The Lord's heart towards children was tender. I'm sure he had a kindness, a countenance, even a sweet sense of humor that made them love him, draw near to him, and feel safe by his side.

I pray that we, as Christians, would not necessarily cause the world to say "Can she be ours?" but rather "Can her God be mine? I want her Lord to go home with me. I don't want to leave without him."

May we be so much like him, may we resemble him so much before the world that the child in everyone is captivated by his love in us.

Father,
   I realize
      how important it is
to stand,
   sit,
      kneel before
         your throne
so that the radiance
   you bestow
      upon me there
         can be used
            to shine on others.

∞

YIELD

❧

But I see another law at work in the members of my body, waging war against the law of my mind and making me a prisoner of the law of sin at work within my members.

Romans 7:23

Often in my journey up the mountains and through the valleys, I want to set up camp. Sometimes it's because of brokenness and weariness; I feel I can't possibly go on, or I don't want to go on, so I stop walking. At other times I sense a wellness, a joy, a peace, and I want to just settle down into a cleft of a rock somewhere—comfortable, secure, content.

I am learning that the only time I can stop walking on this journey home is when I am in a holy resting place. This is a place in which I acknowledge my weariness and frailty, and Jesus is carrying me or I am sleeping in his arms. Knowing I'm yielding to his will and voice, knowing I can't go places where the Holy Spirit has to go, I pray and lay my life in God's hands.

The Bible tells me there is sin at work in my members. It also says that "everyone who has this hope in him purifies himself, just as he is pure" (1 John 3:3). To purify myself is an act of my will. I must be willing to let God do what he wants to do in me. I must be committed to the crushing, surrendered to the surgery, bowed to the breaking.

I have learned that I cannot ask the Lord to have the river of life pour through me and at my core there be a well filled with years of brokenness. I cannot possess the true disposition and character of Jesus—his kindness, gentleness, grace, humility, love, strength, power, and wisdom—when my Christianity means that I only clothe myself with these things and then remove them at night before I go to bed. That is much too superficial.

Certain work must be done. A transforming from glory to glory, where the layers of old emotions and pain are given over to God's truth, and where repentance is a state of heart that I live and put into practice by turning away from sinful patterns and ways. The more I am transformed, the more the old emotions and old ways of relating and thinking will lose their power and die. The holiness of God can then freely come into my feelings, sexuality, thoughts, and identity, and into my ways of speaking, processing, and responding.

We fear going to those very places where we will find freedom. We are petrified at the thought of God touching our hurts, afraid that his touch will cause us to hurt even more. We may even stubbornly and pridefully think we are doing okay or even pretty good—especially if we are well liked or successful. But our popularity or success may not necessarily have come from Jesus. These things can actually smother the life of God in you—the changes the Lord wants to make in you and the growth he longs to see in you and give you.

Let the Lord have his complete way with you. He loves you so much and has far greater plans for you than you can ever have for yourself. And he does make everything beautiful in his time. Allow God to move in you powerfully. Yield to his voice—calling deeper—higher still. He will take you there.

Lord,
   I pray
      that through this life
   I will constantly
      be on a journey
         in
      searching out your heart—
         finding
      treasure
         after treasure ...

FILLED

∞

Come now, let us reason together.
Isaiah 1:18

For months I experienced great anxiety over some career decisions I had to make. Many opinions and much talk about the direction I should take came my way. I wanted to follow my heart, but I wanted it to be God's heart. I decided to take some time to fast and pray.

I've lived on Long Island most of my life. I love having access to New York City about sixty miles away, and I love the ocean, the trees, and the seasons. I reserved a hotel room for a couple of days in Montauk Point, which is the easternmost tip of Long Island. I often hop in my car and take the back roads through the Hamptons to get there. Along the way, I pass many different restaurants, antique stores, quaint little inns, and homemade ice-cream shops. I never tire of the drive.

It was October, and I knew hardly a soul would be out there during the fall season. It would be quiet, which would make it easier for me to focus on hearing God. Since the days were growing cooler, I packed a couple of sweaters and then loaded a bag with my Bible, some books, legal pads, pens, and cassettes. It was me and God—I was on a mission. I had prayed that he would truly meet me during this time.

Halfway through my trip, over the music blaring in my tape deck, God spoke to my spirit. "Shut the music off. I want you to sing to me. Please sing to me." My hand reached for the power button and I drove in silence. I wept at the Lord's gesture, at his beckoning for me to worship him. My voice filled the car:

"Great is thy faithfulness, Oh God, my Father, there is no shadow of turning with thee. Thou changest not, thy compassions, they fail not; as thou hast been, thou forever wilt be . . . Jesus, Jesus, Jesus, there is something about that name. Master, Savior, Jesus . . . Change my heart, Oh God, make it ever true. Change my heart, Oh God, may I be like you . . ."

I sang and I sang. I cried. And cried some more. He was preparing me for my time with him. He was filling me with his peace and the certainty of his presence. The following three days were sweet and serene. I wrote and I read and I prayed. I received some answers to my prayers, gained some wisdom, and grew closer to him.

If we would just take time with him . . . make time for him. Not just surviving with Jesus, but thriving with Jesus. Pursuing him as he pursues us. We would be so much more in tune with what his desires are for us. We would be so much more filled with the Spirit, transformed by the renewing of our minds, and changed. We do not necessarily have to embark on a three-day trip, although that was precious to me and I will never forget it. But it can be whatever we make it to be—a drive, a fifteen-minute rendezvous at sunrise, a walk, a certain place to retreat during the day, a quiet break just before sleep. We must not lose sight of him, we must not grow numb to his voice, we must not ever let our lives revolve around ourselves so completely that the One who longs to meet us is left waiting.

You, Lord,
   are a brilliant, radiant, burning flame,
   glowing with colors
      that warm my soul.
You, Lord,
   are the fireside
I will sit by
   for all eternity.

∞

EEING JESUS

∞

If we claim to have fellowship with him yet walk in the darkness, we lie and do not live by the truth.

1 John 1:6

$\mathscr{I}$ fly all the time. I don't like to. As a matter of fact, I hate it. But I know it would be impossible for me to set up a satellite dish and sing from my living room. So off I go.

They announced the flight would be full, so I was relieved to get settled into my seat before most of the passengers had boarded. I sat and watched them as they made their way to their seats—the many different faces, different destinations, different stories behind each of their lives. My thoughts were interrupted by a flight attendant who caught my attention in a way few had. An undeniable radiance exuded from her person. I was sure she was a Christian—the way she smiled, the way she showed patience, kindness, and grace to everyone she encountered.

Halfway through the flight I got up to use the rest room. The flight attendant was sitting in the back of the plane, and while I'd never done anything like this before, somehow I had to ask her . . . My question wasn't as standard as "Are you a Christian?" No, it was much more direct. I even surprised myself as I asked, "You love Jesus, don't you?"

She looked up at me, and with a glow in her eyes, she said, "Yes, how did you know?"

I told her I had watched her and that her actions and her countenance spoke loudly to me about her love for him.

The river of life inside of that flight attendant splashed onto everyone around her. And if she had never spoken a word that day, all those coming in contact with her would have seen clearly the God of the universe living inside of her heart.

I want to be so filled with his river that everyone around me can dive right in—can be refreshed, cleansed, and awakened to a God who loves them like no other. I want to live in such a way that those I encounter will experience the most impacting introduction of their lives. May they meet Jesus.

Smiles—
  gentle,
    warm,
      little gestures
  reaching out,
    touching,
      communicating
        in
          a quiet,
            tender,
              soft way.
Lord,
  let my smile
    always
  be an invitation
    for all
      to
    meet its source.

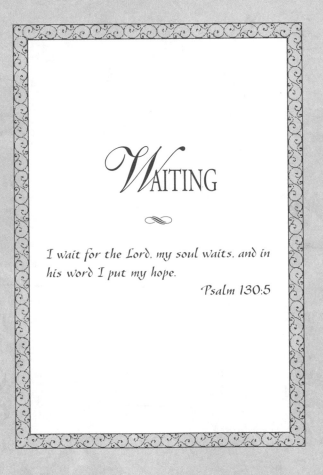

WAITING

I wait for the Lord, my soul waits, and in his word I put my hope.

Psalm 130:5

I want to *do*. I want to *say*. I want to *act*. I'm so guilty of getting in the way of God's timing. To learn to wait has been so difficult for me. I want to "fix" things quickly: the comment someone said about me; the comment I said about someone; the sudden news that turns my whole world upside down; the misunderstanding; the wanting to prove my point or the validity of my character; the uncomfortable changes life often brings.

I would like God to involve himself in my circumstance according to my timing and my agenda. I forget how holy and perfect his ways, his timing, and his agenda are. Yet, over and over I see that when I wait, letting him be God, then he *is* God.

He comes in ways I would have never imagined—moving heaven and earth to work out his heart and will in my life. He often prepares me for encounters with others that are healing and peaceful because I wait to speak. In instances of gossip, when I've wanted to defend myself and didn't, the Lord went before me. According to Isaiah 54:17, "No weapon forged against you will prevail, and you will refute every tongue that accuses you." Those who needed to hear the truth, heard the truth.

As changes take place in my life, I continue to watch them truly work out for my good—if I can just wait on God to see me through. What makes all the difference is trust—the understanding that God has a much bigger plan than mine even if I don't understand it. I'm grateful, yet sorry, that I have had to learn so many lessons by hindsight.

The circumstances of life can embitter any of us at any time. But if we allow it, God's grace and love can empower us and help us move through these times victoriously. As Oswald Chambers says, "It is not our circumstance, but God in our circumstance."

More and more, I'm learning to embrace what life has to offer, to soak the poison out of it by taking in God's love in a way that helps me do, act, and say exactly what is in *his* heart to do, act, and say. And I only become a better woman for it. My heart continues to grow wider so that more of Jesus can dwell in me. I'm reminded of Romans 5:3–5, "We also rejoice in our sufferings, because we know that suffering produces perseverance; perseverance, character; and character, hope. And hope does not disappoint us, because God has poured out his love into our hearts by the Holy Spirit, whom he has given us."

Oh Father,
	as David has said,
	"All my longings lie open
		before you:
	my sighing is
		not hidden from you."
Maker of my heart,
	you know me
	better than
		I know myself—
	my emotional swings,
		feelings,
			anxieties,
				fears.
Lord, I trust you
	with it all—
	to help me weigh things,
		balance,
	look at life
		in the light
			of your perspective.
And like David,
	"I wait for you, O Lord.
		You will answer, O Lord,
			my God."
For you, Jesus,
	have never failed me.
You know my needs
	and meet them.
Oh God,
	grow me up in you.

∞

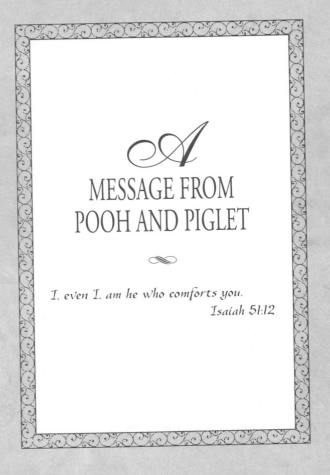

A
MESSAGE FROM
POOH AND PIGLET

I, even I, am he who comforts you.
Isaiah 51:12

I love greeting cards—the way they make me feel when I receive them and when I give them: tokens of kindness, reminders of love, offers of thanksgiving. We exchange greetings at the traditional times: birthdays, holidays, anniversaries. And then there are those wonderful "for nothing" times—unexpected words from the heart. Sometimes tender, sometimes funny, these sweet gifts show up in a mailbox or on a windshield, in a book or a suitcase, or amidst a bouquet of flowers.

My personal favorites are the ones that are blank inside. I appreciate the opportunity to express my feelings for someone in a way that uniquely fits that person or the situation in that person's life. However long or short—writing our feelings down and sending them to our loved ones is always worth the time and energy. It's amazing what often transpires. Smiles, tears, hugs, encouragement, healing. Cold walls melt, hard days take an easier turn, and bitterness gives way to forgiveness. The saying that life is far too short and unpredictable is absolutely true. I try not to let a day go by without saying what needs to be said—or even what needs to be said again.

I love to haunt old bookstores, antique shops, floral stores, and quaint little restaurants with a section of one-of-a-kind cards. I remember the day I picked up one that showed Winnie the Pooh and Piglet on the front walking hand in hand. Their conversation went like this:

"Pooh?" Piglet said.

"Yes, Piglet."

"Oh, nothing," Piglet said. "I just wanted to be sure of you."

I stared at it awhile, smiled, and then read it a few more times. I've asked this question of close friends at many different times in my life, in many different ways. I need the safety, the reassurance, the knowing they are right there and that I am loved.

So often my daily experiences remind me of my relationship with Jesus. The simplicity of that exchange between Pooh and Piglet mirrors an almost daily conversation between God and myself: "Jesus?" I say.

"Yes, Kathy."

"Oh, nothing," I say. "I just wanted to be sure of you."

The mention of his name. My protector. My deliverer. My shelter. My Lord. My comfort. My reason for being. If I can be sure of anything, I can be sure of him.

It was a weeping day yesterday . . .
   On
      and off,
   tears fell uncontrollably.
Little girl
   that I truly am—
      couldn't be held enough,
         couldn't be told
   I was loved enough,
   couldn't quite believe enough.
And yet,
   as I looked to you,
      Lord,
   I knew that
      you were holding me,
         loving me,
            believing for me.

⚮

BECOMING IRRESISTIBLE

❧

In love he predestined us to be adopted as his sons through Jesus Christ, in accordance with his pleasure and will—to the praise of his glorious grace, which he has freely given us in the One he loves.

Ephesians 1:4-6

"Coli . . . Coli . . ." Logan called softly as he came up the stairs to wake me up. His mother has called me by that nickname for years. It sounded so sweet coming from her two-year-old's lips.

I was visiting them in Fort Wayne, Indiana. I hadn't seen Logan in a while; spending three days with him was a special treat.

"Hi, Coli . . . Coli . . . hi . . ." His smile extended ear to ear, and his fat cheeks bunched up, reducing his eyes to tiny slits.

"Good morning, Logan," I said. "Whatcha doin'?"

"Donstair. Donstair." He reached for my hand and began tugging me out of bed. The smell of syrup on his face made me want to eat him up. That round belly and plump inner thigh were totally squeezable. I have no qualms about taking advantage every chance I get. I am mesmerized by Logan's chuckle, the sound of his voice, his innocence. At that age, kisses are endless and hugs happen every five minutes. I loved watching his excitement at the sight of his mom and dad. Every time they came into the room or passed by for something Logan announced with a glow, "Mommy, Daddy," as if he was showing them off or telling me, "Don't miss this."

By mid-morning Logan sat in his high chair, and we all sang lullabies. He fought his tiredness, but finally succumbed to a sleep that gently fell over him as the music filled the room. I leaned towards him. He rested his head on my shoulder as I whispered the tail end of the songs that brought him peace.

It was at that moment I realized that I wanted to be just like Logan. To have people so taken by my joy, my innocence, and my excitement about my Father. To be so given over to God that all I am reflects my upbringing by him. Jesus: I want to show him off in the holiest sense. When I walk into a room, I want the Holy Spirit to say, "Don't miss this."

We are born of God. May we never lose our zeal over that. May we never take for granted our adoption as his sons and daughters. We are children of the King.

Sweet
  Husband
    Jesus,
  may
    this bride
      wake up
        every morning,
          more eager
        and more excited
            than the day before,
        with
        the thought
      of new ways
        to serve you,
          to please you.

                    ∞

MOVING GOD'S HEART

❧

But when you pray, go into your room, close the door and pray to your Father, who is unseen. Then your Father, who sees what is done in secret, will reward you.

Matthew 6:6

When I take a moment to silence myself before God, his words to me and my prayers to him are some of the sweetest, most comforting times in my life. Mother Teresa has said that the first requirement for prayer is silence, and that people of prayer are people of silence. I have discovered it's in those silent times that the Lord gives me his heart to pray for myself . . .

Continue to heal me of my many broken places.

Continue to pour your rightness into my emotions.

Continue to work your will in me so that I only walk in places you have prepared for me.

Continue to restore the years the locust have eaten— either by what was handed to me or by what I chose in rebellion.

Continue to work in me a softness, a sweetness, a grace that only a woman in love with you can possess.

Continue to help me endure others' injustices with a heart of forgiveness.

Wrap your heart around my heart in such a way that all that is you becomes me.

Invade me with your love so deeply that all the poisons of bitterness and hatred are driven out.

Allow me to be feminine, kind, and gentle.

Continue to bring healing and wholeness to my body, soul, spirit, and mind.

Allow me to possess an understanding heart, a discerning spirit, a compassionate soul—and a mind full of wisdom.

May I love—deeply, fully, richly—not with a love that comes from a human place, but from your heart of holiness, purity, and righteousness.

Continue to allow me to possess a joy that comes from heaven—that gives me strength to face whatever life has to offer.

May I be disciplined and self-controlled.

May I pick up my cross daily and exercise the willingness and obedience to follow you—whatever the cost.

May I possess an unwavering faith and put my hope in your work and your promises.

Continue to remind me of the things you say about me, and help me to believe you and rest in you.

May I always know how much you love me.

Thousands of words to pray. Thousands of times he hears. Infinite ways he comes. Prayer moves the heart of God.

Let me
   always
      go inside
         my closet,
      shut the door,
         exposing
            all my heart
               to you—
         good and bad—
            in this
               quiet, secret place.
'You listen,
   you forgive,
      you teach,
         you love me tenderly
      as we share,
so when I open the door,
   and step
      outside
   into this world,
      I can
         freely,
            naturally,
            and confidently
               introduce
               the world
               to you.

✀

$\mathcal{M}$Y
FIRST LOVE

❧

Like a lily among thorns is my darling among the maidens.

Song of Songs 2:2

On Nantucket Island, off the coast of Massachusetts, it was a cloudy, windy day. Cobblestones lined the main street, and small shops and restaurants were attached together with old-fashioned elegance. As I passed them, I knew each had a story to tell. I could almost hear faraway voices from long ago places beckoning. I couldn't help but feel in every sense Nantucket's romantic atmosphere; I felt its embrace, and I longed to share it with someone I loved.

While it was a fairy tale atmosphere, the damp breeze blowing in from the shore was real enough. As I returned to the inn where I was spending the night, I felt that deep familiar longing. I closed my door and fell to my knees. I thought how much I would love to be strongly but gently held at that moment. Like so many other times, I tearfully expressed my feelings, and God listened. "You alone can fill me with the peace and comfort I need right now. I believe you see the depths of my heart. Every turn, every corner—every cry. You can meet my every need." There was a long silence, then my voice broke through the quiet. "I realize you were right beside me today. *You* put me in an environment I loved and my desire to be in love was met in a very unique way. In a way I hadn't expected. *You*, Jesus, are the man in my life. You've been here all along. *You* are my beloved. *You* are the One I have betrothed my life to. You've granted me this day and the sweetness of your presence."

As I listened to myself pray, I was reminded of my covenant with him—intimacy with him. Marriage or not, Jesus will always be my bridegroom. Always be my first love. I realized that we had a memory-making day together and that he had lavishly given me many of the kinds of things I cherish. I truly am in the midst of a love affair that will last for all eternity.

You are his bride. You are his love. What a romantic God we serve. "I belong to my lover, and his desire is for me" (Song of Songs 7:10). Don't ever forget the place you have with Jesus. It is a place that is reserved for you and you alone—so close to his heart that on some days if you close your eyes and listen intently, you may hear his very breath. It is his breath that continually breathes life into your soul. You are so deeply loved. Walk arm and arm with him today. Your eternal escort. Your faithful bridegroom. He will never let you go.

Your
    left hand
        under my head
    and your
        right hand
            embracing me,
        as this
            bride
                rests
        in a
                cushion of love—
                    breathing out quietly,
                rejoicing with
                    peaceful sighs.
    Knowing
        the One
            who holds her
        is
            her maker
        and her
                forever husband.

❧

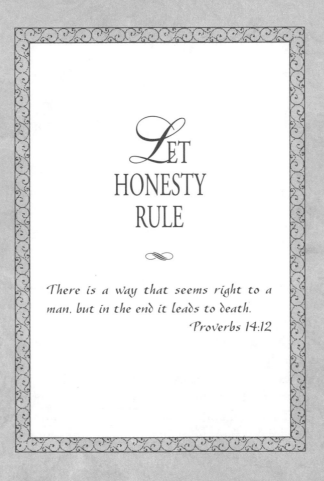

*L*ET
HONESTY
RULE

∽

There is a way that seems right to a
man, but in the end it leads to death.

Proverbs 14:12

There I was in this huge room at the Metropolitan Museum of Art in New York City. The surrounding paintings were magnificent and left me in complete awe of the talent God bestows upon mankind. Some were so finely detailed that these stunning portraits and scenes made me wonder: "Are they breathing . . . I could bet on the fact that that eye was following me . . . She'll speak to me any minute now." So real. So beautiful. I walked slowly through each room, not wanting to miss any of the genius before me.

Above one of the arched doorways hung a painting of Adam and Eve. One figure lay on one side of the tree of good and evil and one lay on the other. The serpent, wrapped tightly around the trunk of the tree, cunning and sly, his ominous presence filled the painting. I could almost hear the conversation that day in the garden.

God told Adam and Eve that they were free to eat from any tree, save for the tree of the knowledge of good and evil. If they ate of that one, they would surely die. (See

Genesis 2:16–17.) I let my eyes focus on this unique interpretation of the first man and woman: The serpent, cool and crafty, leaning over to Eve, saying, "Did God really say 'You must not eat from any tree in the garden?'" Then snickering, "*Surely* you will not die."

"Did God really say it?" "Are you sure?" "Surely he didn't." How often I am tempted to listen to those words—how often all of us are. God most definitely has spoken. His word, steadfast and unchanging, he means what he says. Does what he says. Never pulls a fast one. And still we question or disregard his heart. I, for one, have indulged in the rationalizing, the putting a stamp of "okay" on something that God has said is unholy. We need only look around today to see the effects of Satan's questions. Moral and spiritual decay. A rightness placed on what is so obviously wrong. A label of old-fashioned and barbaric attached to laws that are still the same in God's eyes and that he still cherishes. A bend toward our own philosophies. A turning from absolute truth to what our own truth happens to be.

So we are left believing the lies of the enemy and with the consequences of our choices. And it all takes place under the guise of love and honesty, goodness and fairness, open-mindedness and tolerance.

The serpent may come to you and say, "Did God really say that?" Your answer must be "yes". "For no matter how many promises God has made, they are 'Yes' in Christ" (2 Corinthians 1:20). "Yes!" to all he desires and "No!" to all he does not. Nothing is worth being out of the will of God. Take him at his word.

Thank you
    so much, Lord,
for teaching me
        about myself,
        about my heart,
for constantly
    challenging me
        to see what's there.
Let me be
    true to you,
        true to myself.
Let honesty
    rule my life,
    and deception
        never be a part of me.
As I continue
        to be open
    and vulnerable
        before you,
    please use me to
        cause people
        to open up their hearts
    to you
        and to
            themselves.

∞

A
BABY'S PRAYER

When I was woven together in the depths of the earth, your eyes saw my unformed body.

Psalm 139:15-16

I long to be a woman of faith. I long to be a Christian filled with the knowledge of God, to possess the substance that will enable me to deliver his heart through my actions. I also want to be an educated believer. Educated in the sense that I do not walk blindly in my faith to the point of not truly seeing what is happening in the world—what people are saying or doing. I don't want to offer pat "Christian answers" to challenging conversations, thoughts, and experiences. I want to use "God's grid," to not be too quick with my opinion, but to allow Jesus to sift his truth through me on any given matter. I must know what I'm talking about and be able to back it up with as much absolute, bottom-line wisdom, discernment, and truth that I could only receive from the mind and heart of God. I try to practice this daily in all areas, but one particular area comes to mind.

Realizing I wanted to learn more about the abortion issue in this country, I took a six-week course in the most important aspects of the issue. I have a tender heart for the unborn, and I knew just having an opinion wasn't enough. So I watched videos, listened to interviews, and read documents and statistics. The more educated I became, the more horrified I became.

Right after I completed the course, I performed a concert in Oregon. I spoke boldly that night, more strongly than ever before, on this particular topic. My spirit grieved within me. But then, as I climbed into bed that evening, I found myself wondering whether I had come off too strongly and offended people. Had I gone ahead of God? I asked the Lord to forgive me if I'd spoken out of turn. When I finally fell asleep, it was with a bit of a heavy heart.

Four years later, I returned to that same city. As I signed autographs and talked to as many people as were willing to wait, I noticed a young woman standing over to the side. After everyone left, she approached me. "Kathy," she said, "I had to wait to speak with you. You were here four years ago and spoke out for the unborn." As she spoke, a small child with bouncing blond hair ran to me and wrapped her tiny arms around my neck. "I was going to have an abortion that week," the woman went on. "I want to thank you for what you said that night. This is my little miracle," she finished, drawing the little girl close to her.

Oh, how I want to be about life—because God is about life. Don't you think it's amazing that the Lord chose an unborn baby, John the Baptist, to be one of the first to proclaim the coming of the Messiah?

With all of the militancy around this volatile issue, I decided that a prayer from a baby's heart would extend a gentle mercy and forgiveness. So, for all who need to hear, for all who carry a heavy cloud of guilt, for all who will make a choice, for all who need healing, this is for you . . .

I can hear her talking with a friend
I think it's all about me
Oh, how she can't have a baby now
My mommy doesn't see.
That I feel her breathe
I know her voice
Her blood it flows through my heart
God, you know my greatest wish is that
We'd never be apart.
But if I should die
Before I wake
I pray her soul you'll keep
Forgive her, Lord, she doesn't know
That you gave life to me.
Do I really have to say good-bye
Don't want this time to be through
Oh, please tell her that I love her, Lord
And that you love her, too.
Cause if I should die
Before I wake
I pray her soul you'll keep
Forgive her, Lord, she doesn't know
That you gave life to me.
On the days when she may think of me
Please comfort her with the truth
That the angels hold me safe and sound
Cause I'm in heaven with you
I'm in heaven with you . . .

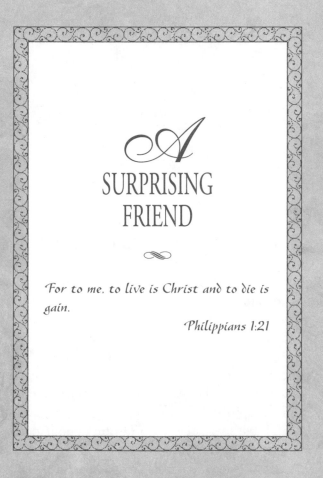

A
SURPRISING
FRIEND

For to me, to live is Christ and to die is gain.

Philippians 1:21

Cardinal Joseph Bernardin was a respected and holy man. He lived in Chicago and served humanity with a steadfast display of the character of God. This humble servant was stricken with cancer and held an amazing demeanor and stoic nature at the end of his life. He was portrayed gallantly by the media. I'm always so thankful for lives in such surrender to Jesus. I read a quote by the Cardinal that was significant to me: "You have the choice to make death either your friend or your enemy. I choose to make it my friend." He was talking about the state of his body on this, his last earthly journey, but his statement has a greater spiritual significance.

The Bible speaks clearly and often about death—a "dying to self," and a "denying of one's self" in order that all that Christ is may live in us. Galatians 2:20 tells us, "I have been crucified with Christ and I no longer live, but Christ lives in me." Philippians 3:10 says, "I want to know Christ and the power of his resurrection and the fellowship of sharing in his sufferings, becoming like him in his death …" In Luke 9:23, Jesus says, "If anyone would come after me, he must deny himself and take up his cross daily and follow me." A daily death. A daily choosing to pick up the cross. This represents many different things in each of our lives. Who wants to go through the dying process? Yet, without the crucifixion, there would have been no resurrection; without death, no life—without suffering, no glory.

We can hold on to things and stay in places of brokenness. We can go on in ways that are false in healing and false in peace. And, in doing so, we can suffer the tragedy of missing God's heart.

Or we can lay down our lives in celebration to let God do as he wishes with us. I often hear people say, "Why hasn't God come?" or "Why am I still dealing with this?" Many answers to these questions come to mind, and all are had in Jesus. But we are the ones who must put ourselves under the cross so that his blood may pour over our lives. Oftentimes we want to avoid this process. I know I do—only to arrive at a place the Lord has absolutely no part in bringing me to. I look at my person and see holes and flaws that he would gladly fill and fix if I would just surrender and do it his way. Holiness could then have free reign in me.

As the Cardinal so eloquently said, "I choose to make death my friend." The dying process is a strangely sweet reminder of Jesus, and that our present sufferings are not worth comparing with the glory to be revealed in us. Death *can* be our friend if we let it. Pick up your cross, then wait and watch. After each burial, a stone will be rolled away with the mark of another resurrection.

Late January—
    a cool, breezy day—
I decided
    to take a
        long walk
to ease the stirring
    in my heart.
The leaves
    seemed
        to sing out to me
    from
        beneath my feet.
As I
    raised my head,
        I saw
            what seemed like
                endless rows
of tall,
    barren oak trees,
and suddenly
    I heard
        the whisper
of your voice
    amid
        the branches.

You were taking
    my leaves
        of security.
I realized
    how desperately
        I grasped to
            not let go.
But as
    you tenderly
        talked to me,
I knew
    I was being
        stripped
            of myself
and gloriously
blossoming
    to a new growth
        in you.

WHEN YOU NEED HIM MOST

❧

And my God will meet all your needs according to his glorious riches in Christ Jesus.

Philippians 4:19

$\mathscr{J}$m one of those people who can never seem to get warm. In the summer most restaurants feel like meat lockers to me, and in the winter I'm always searching for a sweater, a blanket, a thermostat, or a big old fireplace at which to warm myself. Being on tour in the dead of winter is quite an adventure.

Recently I stayed in a room that was so cold, a dish of ice cream wouldn't melt with the thermostat on high. The ceiling vents were blowing cold air, and so I decided to stand on a chair and close them in hopes of regaining some of the feeling in my hands, feet, and nose. Unfortunately, as I reached for the vent, the chair tumbled forward. I fell onto my side, the wind knocked out of me. I stumbled to the phone to call my road manager. Andrew came and sat with me and propped me against some pillows as I got my breath back. We decided to forgo the emergency room so that we could get on the bus in time to reach the next city by morning. I ached, lost sleep, and was in fairly constant pain when I walked into the next hotel. "Jesus touch me," was my constant prayer.

I'm always amazed at God's hand. So present. So comforting. A woman involved with the concert that day took me to a doctor she knew. I was tired, a little down, and sorry that I wasn't very talkative. She was sweet, bubbly, and very concerned. The Lord was kind to have this dear lady serve me so well. She prayed for me as we drove, and as she did, my weary heart was eager to acknowledge his touch.

The doctor was a gentle man, attentive and sympathetic. He checked me out, told me I had a fractured rib, and gave me the necessary medical advice. Then he focused on Jesus. He talked about Jesus. He bragged about Jesus. His faithfulness. His power. His healing. He asked me if he could pray for me and when I responded positively, offered a precious prayer on my behalf. His words soothed the ache in my side as well as the one in my soul. I was far away from home—no friends, no family—but the Lord met me. He is my home. He is my family. He is my friend. Every situation, every circumstance—he proves himself true. Never a want without him knowing. Never a desire without him seeing. Never a need without him coming to meet it. He will. His way. He promises.

As I close
    my tired eyes
and rest my
        dream-filled head
on a
        soft pillow,
I can
    sleep
        in peace,
    knowing
        that I
        and my future
are in the
    almighty hands
of
    my
        almighty
        God.

HE LEAVES
THE LIGHT ON

∞

I will never leave you nor forsake you.
                              Joshua 1:5

It was one of those rare nights where I could relax and plop myself in front of the television set. Didn't want to work my brain, didn't want to think about anything. I made myself a soothing cup of tea, found the comforter, and reveled in the feeling of soft pillows against my back. I love to watch the old shows, the old movies—the theme songs have a strange way of warming my heart.

As I settled in, I happened upon a once popular weekly series called "The Wonder Years." I'd only watched it a few times before. I'd enjoyed the little I had seen of it, so I thought I'd give it a try. The series revolved around the life of a boy in the sixties; his family, his friends, his school. He narrated each show, but as an adult looking back upon his younger years.

This particular episode was about his sister, a senior in high school. She was going through a rebellious stage, a "finding herself" period. She barely talked to her mom and could hardly converse with her father. Whenever there was even a hint of conversation, it ended up in an argument, frustration, slamming doors, etc. These conflicts accelerated until she finally decided to leave home with some friends. It was her birthday, and earlier that evening her family had gathered in the kitchen to offer a celebration of sorts. The cake was lit, and the birthday song sung with melancholy overtones. Her father handed her his gift with all the tenderness he held in his heart for her. She opened it clumsily and nervously and was taken aback by what she found in her hands—his duffel bag from the army. Their eyes met briefly, but then a horn honking interrupted those seconds of tenderness. She offered an awkward "thanks," hugged everyone, and left.

The next scene showed the front of the house. It was after dark, and the narrator (her brother) was saying, "Even though my father didn't know when and if my sister would ever come home, he kept the porch light on for her every night." And with those words, the light next to the front door flashed on.

I thought of Jesus. His love for me. Tears of thankfulness drenched my face as I fell on my knees. A rebellious daughter whose Father keeps the porch light on—never giving up on her, always holding out hope she will come home. Always open-armed, always ready to receive, always offering me a place where love has no bounds. Bless you, Father.

It amazes me
   how you never
      get tired
   of hearing
      the same cries
         pour
         out of me.
My thoughts
   ramble on
      and
      you listen,
         listen ...
Discouragement
   within myself
weighs
   me down,
   but you continually
      lift it
         from me.
Frustration
      builds,
      but you tear it down.

Hurt
   pierces
      the depths
         of my
            heart,
but you
   soothe it,
      heal it
by
      living there.
Thank you
   for being
      Lord of my life,
      hearer of
            my prayers,
hope
   for tomorrow.
Thank you
   for being
      my Father.

FRESH MERCY

❦

*Because of the LORD's great love we are
not consumed, for his compassions never
fail. They are new every morning; great
is your faithfulness.*

Lamentations 3:22-23

There are often times in my travels when I do not have to rush to a plane to show up somewhere at an appropriate time. Some days I'll have to drive late at night to arrive at the next city on time, or set my alarm at what feels like the middle of the night to leave at a decent hour in the morning. Surprisingly, these times on the road are some of my most precious.

My routine includes a quick room check to make sure I've left nothing behind, preparation of a hot beverage for the ride, and the prayer that my swollen eyes will soon return to normal. I may be in New England on a cool, crisp fall day, when the leaves are parading their colors. Some days may take me through the Midwest during summer, where farmland stretches way beyond what I can see, and old houses seem painted on the landscape in just the right places as the sun awakens and gently touches the earth with rays of splendor. I could be somewhere on the West Coast, or way down south, or on one of the islands where I can hear all sorts of beautiful sounds from a vast array of birds as they dance over waters touched by light so magnificent it looks as if someone had dropped thousands of diamonds from the sky.

These scenes are endless in my mind. All of them produce the same experience for me—a sense of newness, freshness, peacefulness, stillness, calm—another day, another start. Untouched, clean, ready to experience all that life has to offer once again. I am constantly reminded of the faithfulness of God and that his mercies are new every morning. What I was yesterday, what I felt yesterday, what I did yesterday is covered by his grace. He remembers it no more. He throws it as far as the east is from the west—as I turn, as I repent, as I offer him my sins, my failures, and even the consequences of my choices. There is so much beauty to the morning, and there is so much beauty in a heart filled with the certainty that the Lord has once again come to fill, restore, and heal.

His steadfast love never ceases. His mercies never end.

All you've done
for me …
My faithful,
    compassionate,
    comforting,
    tender,
        all-loving and
            all-giving,
    miracle-worker,
    teacher,
        disciplinarian,
        God.

May praise
be ever on
my lips
and may a continuing
"thank you"
be heard from
my heart.

∞

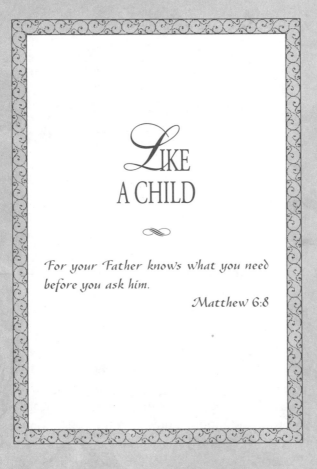

LIKE
A CHILD

∽

For your Father knows what you need before you ask him.

Matthew 6:8

Allyson had just had her second baby, and her two-year-old realized he now had to share his mother and father. Between his confusion and the baby's two hour feedings, Allyson and Brent were totally sleep deprived.

When I arrived for my visit, I was overwhelmed as I watched them cope with their children's constant demands. At the same time, I was blessed by the love and grace I knew the Lord had put in their hearts. They were so self-sacrificing.

I spent most of my time there holding and rocking baby Jordan as he slept—and slept some more. One night as I sat in the living room with him, Allyson finally took a tiny break and plopped down on the couch next to me. She picked up Jordan and laid him on her lap. He began to whimper and she said, "Coli, it's incredible how quickly my milk lets down at the sound of his cry. Isn't God amazing—the way he made us?"

Yes, God is amazing. As a childless woman, experiences like this stay with me awhile. I think about them, digest them, and marvel often at the works of God. Right now I can only appreciate motherhood from the outside looking in, just like Allyson can only appreciate my life—the traveling, the concerts, etc.—from afar. But we do hold this in common: We are his daughters and he delights in us. Where our love ends, his is just beginning.

I watch Allyson's heart and body respond to Jordan's cries. How much more does everything within God Almighty respond to the cries of his children. While we may not understand the reasons for everything we must endure in this life, receiving him like a child and letting him be God is the safest, best, and most comforting place to be. He sees our tears, he wipes them dry, and he delivers everything in his power to meet our greatest needs. He *is* trustworthy.

What
    an
        incredible
            God you are—
never,
        ever
        ceasing to amaze me.
You
    bless,
        and bless,
            and then
                bless me
                    again.
How can
        I ever
        express my love
            for you,
            but by
                allowing
                    my life
to be a blessing
        to you?

≈

THE QUEEN OF BRUISES

∞

I will give you a new heart and put a new spirit in you: I will remove from you your heart of stone and give you a heart of flesh.

Ezekiel 36:26

Years ago, in the early eighties, I lived with a family in Nashville. I stayed in a room above their garage while I started my recording career. Nashville wasn't nearly as integrated then as it is now, and I had limited experience in dealing with anyone other than New York Italian people. The growing Gospel and Country music industries have since caused a melting pot of musicians to move there from all parts of the country. But I was a little misplaced, to say the least; I felt like Rizzo in *Grease* most of the time. I was thankful for the Harrells' generosity and graciousness during this period of my life.

I remember one morning snuggling with three-year-old Caroline on the couch as we watched cartoons. After awhile, I decided to go to my room and spend some time alone reading and praying. I asked her if there was anything she wanted me to pray for. She looked at me with her big brown eyes. "This," she said, pointing to a bruise on her leg. "And this," she said, pointing to another one on her other leg. As the queen of bruises when I was little, I probably averaged about ten falls a day, so I sympathized with her request. I hugged her and told her I most definitely would pray for her.

When I got to my room I pondered the fact that as a child of God my requests that day were not that much different from Caroline's. Her bruises had landed on her legs, and mine had landed in my heart. The Lord continues to heal and restore the wounded places in me as I allow him access. The process is at times so painful that I want to just ignore it and live my life as best I can. But I do believe that we are as sick as our secrets. The places of hurt we bury deep inside, the wounds that seem to open and close according to the circumstances—these things hinder all that we can become in Jesus, all that he desires for our lives. They affect us both relationally and emotionally. They affect us spiritually and morally.

In Psalm 51:6, the Lord says he desires truth in our inner parts; this is where he can move in power and healing. The psalm goes on to say that he teaches us wisdom in our inmost place. He uproots the bad and pours in his best as we let him.

Don't hide from him. Don't hide from yourself. Jesus is gentle yet strong and will walk you through to victorious beginnings.

You'll be amazed at the miracle you will become.

Lord Jesus,
    how I yearn
to be close to you
    right now—
    examining
        my heart,
confessing
    as you purify,
for I know,
    you've told me—
the pure in heart
    shall
    see God.

∞

TEND
MY
GARDEN

~

They will say, "This land that was laid
waste has become like the garden of Eden."
Ezekiel 36:35

I've heard many different analogies that compared the state of one's heart to the image of a garden—the "garden of my heart," or the "garden of my soul," or the "garden of my life." I recently flipped through some journal pages I'd written years ago. As I read, I was encouraged to see that some difficult and desperate seasons of my life are very much in the past. And yet, some experiences and situations still stare me in the face. Some are still very true in my life. Here is a day's entry . . .

Oh Father, you are gently tearing away the dead weeds surrounding my heart. They were once flourishing bright flowers I had planted with my own hands, but somehow I knew they were destined to fade and die. I was aware I'd planted them in the wrong ground, and that they would be choked and starved by the polluted soil they so desperately tried to grow upon. I planted anyway. No matter how I tried to feed and save them, their foundation was their killer. These particular flowers were all I knew—their fragrance, their color, their shape. And I had gotten so used to walking on this particular soil. I was comfortable with the familiarity of planting everything there.

I hold back from you, Lord. So often I want to prevent you from breaking up ground and pulling up weeds in a garden that isn't meant for me, or isn't your will for me to have. Continue to teach me, Father, to let you dig, when you want to, and how you want to, so that my garden is your garden. If the sound of the shovel brings me to tears, then use those tears as water for the new seeds you are planting. I want flowers to bloom in glowing colors that brilliantly display your grace—each petal opening wide in unashamed, abandoned praise to its Maker. May my obedience be the very life of the flowers in this garden, and may your love be the soil upon which their roots are firmly planted.

I pray nothing grows there that doesn't come from the wellspring of who you are. Most of all, I pray that someday I will kneel before your throne, kiss the hands that tended my garden and place at your feet the bouquet of a life given over to you.

Every bit
of the woman
you'd have me be—
I long
to be.

∞

My LIFE IS IN YOUR HANDS

And you will be my witnesses.

Acts 1:8

I received a call one morning from my sister. She was unusually excited and inquisitive. "Kath, why didn't you tell me the story about the man in prison?"

"Jen, what are you talking about?" I asked.

"Chuck Colson, he spoke about you on his radio show this morning."

Many years before, Chuck Colson had started an organization called Prison Fellowship, an outreach to prisoners, their families, and the victims of crime. I have had the incredible opportunity of going into prisons across the country with this organization to sing and share the gospel.

Jen went on to tell me the following remarkable story.

It happened on a particular night in a maximum security prison in Oregon. I had closed my set with a song I wrote called "My Life Is in Your Hands." This song, I might add, was born out of my own journey of knowing beyond a shadow of a doubt that my life is held by God.

My life is in your hands
My heart is in your keeping
I'm never without hope
Not when my future is with you
My life is in your hands
And though I may not see clearly
I will lift my voice and sing
Cause your love does amazing things
Lord, I know
My life is in your hands . . .

Apparently, a man in the service that evening was contemplating suicide. His wife, who had not called him for months, wanted a divorce. At the edge of despair, the words of my song found their way into his heart in that lonely prison. He approached a prison chaplain and told him he, too, wanted to place his life in the hands of Jesus. He wanted to claim my song as his hope before God for his marriage.

Later that week, I sang at a fund raising dinner in Chicago. At the end of the event, a lady walked up to me, an intent look on her face. "Kathy, that song, 'My Life Is in Your Hands,' it absolutely broke my heart tonight. I have a husband in prison . . ." Incredibly, that woman was the prisoner's wife. She ended up calling him. I understand they are back together again.

Was it anything I did? I believe not. Yes, I sang a song that stirred two hearts in such a way that they moved towards each other. But the truth is that I am an ordinary Italian, New York girl who happens to serve an extraordinary God. I need only attest to his mercy in my life, and he will do the rest.

Say yes to God. Give him permission to use you. Make yourself available to him and watch miracles unfold before your eyes.

All I wish for,
  all I long for
    is to be
      a holy woman.
Thank you, Father,
  that you have released
    the power
      for me to do so,
        and that
everything in this life
    that comes my way—
      the instruments
      that bring joy
        or sorrow—
    is held by your
      divine hands,
        carving the very nature,
      the very heart
        of Jesus
          in me.

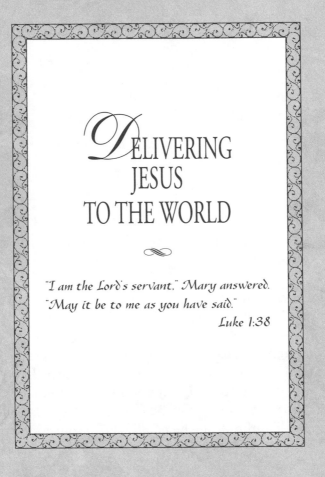

DELIVERING JESUS TO THE WORLD

∞

"I am the Lord's servant," Mary answered.
"May it be to me as you have said."

Luke 1:38

Familiar hymns filled the church as I fell to my knees and received communion that Sunday. I was by myself and grateful for this precious moment alone with God.

It was the Christmas season and many different thoughts about the birth of Christ whirled through my mind. The reality of God being born into a human world—the reality of Christ living in me, dying for me, rising from the dead. It all hit me like a first time revelation. I thought about Mary—her obedience, her willingness, the grace bestowed upon her—a woman honored by God. I longed to be the kind of woman Jesus could delight in—one he could trust. I longed that my heart would be consumed by love for him. I allowed the tears to flow freely. Anytime a yearning, a hunger, a thirst happens inside of me for holiness, I welcome it as my very breath. The words of Mary's prayer mingled with my own . . .

"My soul glorifies the Lord and my spirit rejoices in God my Savior, for he has been mindful of the humble state of his servant . . . for the Mighty One has done great things for me—holy is his name. His mercy extends to those who fear him . . . He has performed mighty deeds with his arm . . . He has filled the hungry with good things" (Luke 1:46–53).

I knew God was listening. I sensed him manifesting his presence to me. These times with him are like nothing else I ever experience on earth. I am always met in his presence. I am always challenged to be like him in his presence. I am always changed in his presence.

Mary heard God. Mary obeyed. Mary delivered Jesus to the world. I whispered my thankfulness to him. I professed my love for him. I cried at the thought of his faithfulness. Softly I said, "Just as Mary delivered your Son to the world, O God—so may I deliver your Son to a desperate world." I long to live a life surrendered to him—a life in relentless pursuit of the things that are his. My body, soul, and spirit—completely his. Once again, I place my life in his hands.

Allow me to know
      the depth of you,
   to incorporate that into
         my whole being.
I desire to be
   a temple for you, Lord,
      for you
         to live through me,
   a walking piece of love,
      so others
            may touch you,
               taste of you,
   experience Jesus
            on this earth.
      Live your life
         over again
         in me.

GOD
IN THE
MOMENTS

Taste and see that the LORD is good.

Psalm 34:8

Some of us lead such busy lives that we can easily miss the Lord when he comes to visit us. In the last couple of years I've really tried to be more aware of God's love in the midst of places and faces. I've found that it is often in the small things—the ordinary moments turned extraordinary—that I recognize his presence and can sense his kindness and tenderness.

I love taking my nieces Maria and Gina to the movies. My sister is pretty strict about snacks—cheese and crackers and fruit—good for you but not much fun. So I love to watch their faces when I tell them to choose any drink or candy to take into the show. Sometimes I even let them pick two or three items. We hug as we stand in line, and I am grateful that my relationship with them is so warm and open. I remember one particular movie as they sat, one on either side of me. Gina reached for my hand, and Maria leaned her head on my shoulder. At that moment I never wanted them to grow up.

My friend Allyson's baby, Logan, seems to have an inner joy that comes straight from heaven. One day as Allyson and I were running errands she left me in the car with him. Every time I turned to look at him he would giggle with such zeal that I wondered whether he could catch his breath. Any sadness I felt that day was washed away as I listened to Logan laugh . . .

I remember the time I was hurrying through a busy airport to get to my gate on time for a connecting flight. A little lonely, a little tired. I came upon a lady in a wheelchair, and amidst the chaos of the hundreds of people rushing around us, my eyes met hers. The sweetest smile appeared on her face. I smiled back, but I knew she would never fully realize how that small gesture had filled my soul.

Some people hate answering machines. But, traveling as much as I do, I find them not only necessary but often comforting. The messages that end with, "Please know I'm praying for you" or "been thinking about you" or "I love you," seem to come at just the right time. Little gifts that soothe my soul at the end of long, difficult days.

I believe that God is in our everyday no matter whether we see him, feel him, or hear him. Many moments occur in our lives which reveal his face, his touch, his voice. Look for him today. He will be found. You will be sweetly surprised at the many ways he surrounds you with his love.

One of my
    most favorite things
        is
    the morning—
breathing in
    a new day.
Oh, Father,
    I pray
        that more and more
    I'll welcome
        and
            meet
        each new day
            with you,
Knowing that's
    where my fullness
    of peace
        and joy
            and righteousness
will always come from.

PERFECT PEACE

∽

*You will keep in perfect peace him whose
mind is steadfast, because he trusts in you.*

Isaiah 26:3

The ocean is a favorite place of mine, and I have been there many times. I love to stare into the darkness of a midnight blue sky and listen to sounds that only the waves can make. I love to breathe in the freshness of the morning air and feel so alive. The soft breezes dance around my face, leaving me refreshed and comforted. I walk miles along the shoreline leaving my footprints in the sand, which are then invaded by an endless ebb and flow of the tide. These moments bring an unspeakable calm coupled with a reflection on all that is good in my life; precious loved ones, treasured relationships, and all I've been blessed with. During these times I can see with a clear mind and heart all the ways God has held my life and walked me through the most violent storms to bring me to a restful place. Even the bad memories—those painful reminders of hurt and disappointment—somehow get covered with sweet forgiveness and a yearning for all to be right and true under the warm blanket of the Lord's mercy.

For it is when my mind is stayed on Jesus, when my eyes look toward eternal things, when my ears listen way beyond the voices of the day, that I hear the ocean sing. But the sound of this ocean is oh, so much deeper, so much wider, so much more divine. I begin to see above and beyond my situation and my circumstances to my Savior—his words, his tenderness, his compassion, his ways. They are not like any other in their ability to reach into my heart. My concerns and worries are far less burdensome at the thought and the sight of him.

The Lord miraculously puts everything into his perspective when my mind and heart are set on all that he is, on all that he's done, on all that he's promised. I become more thankful, I become more hopeful, and most importantly, I am humbled.

He lives and his love is never ending. Look, listen, and hear. God is near. He will bring you perfect peace.

Allow me
  to be still—
    be still
as
    I again
      realize
    that
      I'm sitting
in the warmness
        of
the palm of your hands—
the
    very hands
      that
      will gently unfold
    your
      perfect will
for
    everything
      in my life.

THE DISEASE
OF
COMPARISON

∾

Each one should test his own actions.
Then he can take pride in himself, with-
out comparing himself to somebody else.

Galatians 6:4

We hit cold, hard walls when the disease of comparison invades our life and thinking. I call it a disease because it kills our strength to serve, it dulls our sense of reality, it hardens our hearts. It blurs our ability to see all God has done and can do. A bitter taste lingers in our mouths so that thankful words cannot be uttered. The disease of comparison weakens our souls to the point of exasperation or depression, and we reach for the blanket of self-pity to keep us warm and to comfort us.

The truth is—his will for you is unique. He has made you unique. He has made you to *be* you—no one else. Resist the attitude that causes you to feel sorrow or betrayal because of someone else's gifts or good fortune. Rejoice with those who rejoice. God can come freely into a heart that is generous toward others, with a soul that celebrates the blessings and opportunities others enjoy. He has intentions for you, a destiny that was ordered at the beginning of time, and he will not withhold it. His perspective is eternal. A day is like a thousand years and a thousand years like a day. The Lord is always at work on your behalf, yearning for you to be where *he* desires for you to be. Jeremiah 29:11 tells us, "'For I know the plans I have for you,' declares the LORD, 'plans to prosper you and not to harm you, plans to give you hope and a future.'"

Keep looking to him. Keep trusting in him. Know that he is always leading you to a higher place—let him. The road may look strange to you. You may even feel lost, or far behind, or confused. But if you follow Jesus, it will be the right road, and in the end you will have peace. For peace is found only in the center of God's will. "However, as it is written: 'No eye has seen, no ear has heard, no mind has conceived what God has prepared for those who love him'" (1 Corinthians 2:9).

God, my Father,
   I pray
      that my heart
      may truly rejoice
         with those
            who rejoice
      and truly mourn
         with those
            who mourn.
   Let my heart grow pure,
      tender,
   filled with compassion,
      trusting you
         with every person,
      every circumstance,
         as well as
            my own.

FEELING FORGOTTEN

He has also set eternity in the hearts of men; yet they cannot fathom what God has done from beginning to end.

Ecclesiastes 3:11

Copper-gold sunlight pierced the green leaves, and deep tones of green, burgundy, and brown emanated from the painting on the wall. Written on the bottom of this picture were the words of Eccleciastes 3:1: "To everything there is a season, and a time to every purpose under heaven" (KJV). I continued to stare at the painting as God's Word continued to fall over me like a warm blanket. "He has made everything beautiful in its time" (Ecclesiastes 3:11), and also, "For the revelation awaits an appointed time. . . . Though it linger, wait for it; it will certainly come and will not delay" (Habakkuk 2:3).

So often I question the Lord. I wonder where he is and when he's going to do something. I grumble and complain, mistaking the severe mercy of God for neglect. I feel forgotten and ignored. I think my prayers are falling on deaf ears, when all the while he is listening. He is seeing far and deep, often protecting me from my wants, waiting for my maturity to catch up with my desires. He is patient as my longings mellow to the point where I won't hurt myself and as I learn to desire his will more than mine.

Why is it so difficult for us to understand that God only wants the best for us? Why is it so hard to take him at his word? He's never lied to us. He never will lie to us. His promises can never be broken. They have withstood the test of time.

Next time you think you hear nothing in response to your prayers, don't assume God isn't listening. He may simply want you to rest in his shadow until he reveals his answer. When you hear a direct no, remind yourself there will always be a better yes. God is for you, and he will work out everything in conformity with the purpose of his will. (See Ephesians 1:11.) Everything.

I pray for you and for myself—that we will both grow in our faith. That the times we doubt God will grow fewer and fewer and that the eyes of our hearts will be enlightened. That we may know God's goodness, real and solid, even in the darkness. May we come to realize that God is motivated by a love so strong, so undying, and so wise that we have nothing and no one to fear. He only wants the best, and his best is ours to have. Wait for it.

Expectations
 placed upon me
   by
     my own self.
consuming me
instead of
 your timing,
   your working,
     your creating.
I want
 a
     perfect,
       godly
         woman
         all at once.
My timing
 is either
     too early
     or late,
my working
 often
     overly done,
       or not done enough,
 and
     my creating
       only a
         very cheap
           picture
         taking the place
           of what can be
         your very own masterpiece.

∞

THROUGH EVERY VALLEY

~

Even though I walk through the valley of the shadow of death. I will fear no evil. for you are with me: your rod and your staff. they comfort me.

Psalm 23:4

I waited in the lobby of Sloan Kettering Hospital for word of my mother's condition. She had conquered breast cancer two years before and was now undergoing surgery to remove a tumor in her liver.

I looked around the crowded room; others waited, just as I did, for some word about their loved ones. Nurses would appear every so often with news. You could hear relieved sighs and cries of grief all at the same time. I paced and prayed and wondered when Mom would be done.

Finally, over the loudspeaker, my name was called. With a great deal of uneasiness, I made my way to the desk, where a receptionist handed me a phone. "Kathy, there wasn't just *one* tumor," my mother's doctor began, "but multiple cancerous tumors throughout your mother's liver." A short silence followed, then, "I'm sorry. There's not much we can do."

"What does this mean?" I asked.

"Six months to two years," he answered.

I felt faint as so many emotions found their way through every part of my body. I thought about my dad, who died of colon cancer at forty-six years old. I thought about my mom's suffering. I thought about being orphaned.

I walked through the lobby toward a small chapel. No one was in the room, and I fell across one of the pews—face down, on my stomach. The sound of my weeping filled the room. Then, in my mind, I found myself looking out over a mountaintop; one side was full of all I'd known Jesus to be, and the other side was a valley of voices rising in chorus: "What's the use?" the voices asked. "Just come, eat, drink, and die." I sobbed, moving from anger, to confusion, to helplessness. Then, to my surprise, God's voice seemed to break through it all like lightning through a pitch black sky:

"Am I not still God?"

"Am I not *still* God?"

I laid there motionless, and my breathing was quieted. I knew I could not get up without a response to God's voice. "Yes Lord," I spoke into the hush that had fallen over the chapel, "you are still God."

I prayed then, not for a miracle, but that the Lord would give my mother the needed strength and my sister and myself the kind of heart that would be able to offer her Jesus during this time. I asked him to grant us the gift of his presence and to help us not lose sight of him. I knew it was his grace alone that caused me to even be able to make such a request.

The whole dying process that year, ironically enough, was filled with Jesus' life. He met us at every turn—not without agonizing tears, questions, and long painful days—but he was there. Through the cards, the letters, the talks, the people, the prayers, and the undeniable dauntlessness and graciousness bestowed upon my mother—Jesus was in the midst of it all. During the final hours of her life, I read her Psalm 23 as she took deep breaths to recite it with me. She then led a room full of family and friends in the Lord's prayer.

It sobers me when I think of how this life is only a mist and what *do* we really have besides him? My mother passed, not from death to death, but from life to life—and I've learned that with every death God allows to enter our lives, there *will* come a resurrection. We will only learn the answers when we see him face to face and understand as he understands, but we do have the assurance now of a God who is alive and who is willing and able to carry us through anything. He will surround you with the holy peace of his presence during your deepest sorrows. Be still.

With
   Your unfailing
      lifeline of love,
   You, Lord,
      pull me through
         any situation.

∞

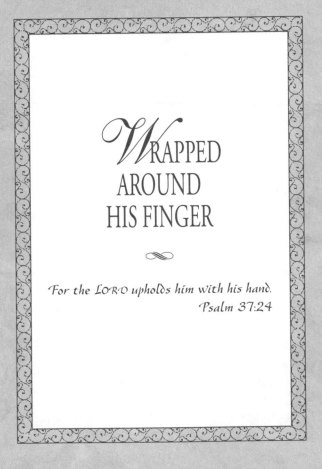

WRAPPED
AROUND
HIS FINGER

❧

For the LORD upholds him with his hand.
Psalm 37:24

Another crazy day. Running around wishing I had more hours to get things done. My mind filled with an endless list—everything I should do, had to do, and wanted to do. I asked myself that all-too-familiar question: "Will life ever slow down? Will the list ever get smaller, or the days get longer?" Too many responsibilities, too many deadlines, too many decisions. The days roll so quickly one into the other. I can never quite catch up. If only I could pay somebody to do my life for me—a twenty-four-hour servant available on call. Or maybe a week's vacation in the sun would do it—once a month, just for a little rest and relaxation. I can imagine. I can dream. Can't I?

Anyway, I spent most of this particular day driving here and there in an effort to get something accomplished. I stopped for a traffic light, and a little girl and her dad walked across the street in front of my car. She wore bright red overalls, and her black silky hair flowed down her back. Her small white sneakers kept pace with her father's strides. I smiled when I saw her tiny hand wrapped tightly around one of her father's fingers; I remembered doing the same with my father. In that moment, I longed to be a child again.

I drove on, thinking about my current frenzy to get things done—a woman on the go but still God's child. A sense of safety, of well-being, of security came over me, and I wrapped my hand around God's finger. He always has my best interest at heart. He knows exactly where I am. He notices everything. The Scriptures tell me, "He will accomplish what concerns me." He sees what frazzles, frightens, and frustrates me.

I took a deep breath as I remembered who I belonged to—and what was really important. That little girl walked beside her father, and I walk beside my God. I'll rest today. I'll trust today. I'll put my hand in his.

I walk
    through
        my life
with
    such a peace
        in
        my heart
and such
        a freedom
            in
            my soul,
when
        I walk
    through my life
            in
        total obedience to you.

∽

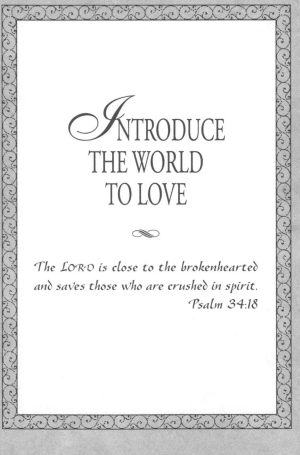

INTRODUCE THE WORLD TO LOVE

*The LORD is close to the brokenhearted
and saves those who are crushed in spirit.*

Psalm 34:18

I noticed the rough, hard-looking teenager at the very beginning of the concert. I somehow knew the walls surrounding her were only a facade. Beyond them was a hurting, lonely little girl—yearning to be held, yearning to be loved. At the conclusion of the concert, head down, she approached me. "I'd really like to talk to you," she said.

The Jesus in me rose up immediately and reached out toward this desperate soul. This precious girl needed the Savior's tender touch.

I finished talking with the others who were lined up, all the while keeping my eye on her. After the church emptied out, a quietness settled over the huge room, and I sat down beside this teenager. I gave her all of my attention, longing for her to know she had all of God's attention and that his mercy would provide a safe place for her to unload her troubles.

The pain then began to pour out of her mouth: ". . . placed in lots of foster homes through the years . . . seventeen years old ... alcoholic ... drug-user ... abused ... parents were gone a lot ... partying's a way of life ..." She didn't know anything about Jesus. She didn't know what he did for her on the cross. She didn't know about his love.

"We all hurt and go through so much in this life," I explained. "But you know what? Jesus hurt more than anyone who ever lived, and he died for you." I continued to share with her about God's love, and she listened with an innocence that penetrated my soul. Finally, I lifted up her face and asked her to look at me. She struggled to meet my eyes. I knew she had seen and experienced a life way beyond her years. Tears were beginning to moisten the deep, dry, dark circles around each of her eyes. "He loves you," I went on. "He loves you."

After our brief exchange of words and a moment of quiet, her heart, in its fragile state of suffering, opened up and invited Jesus in to live and make his home there. She held tightly onto me, and she began to weep even more. Gigantic droplets. I knew Jesus was catching every one of them. *Keep her heart close to you, Lord,* I prayed silently. *Thank you for this incredible opportunity to help this confused and torn life to experience you.*

So many lost. So many broken. So many longing for love from the only one who can give it unconditionally. Hungry souls are everywhere. Be watchful. Remain open. He will fill your eyes with compassion, your words with wisdom, and your heart with mercy. Introduce the world to love. Introduce the world to Jesus.

Lord,
  May
    I always hold
      fragile hearts
  as
    sensitively
    and
      tenderly
    as you do.

$\mathcal{I}$NTO
THE LIGHT

❧

*"For my thoughts are not your thoughts,
neither are your ways my ways," declares
the LORD.*

Isaiah 55:8

It was a hard week, and I was exhausted. My mind was on overload and filled with anxiety as I thought about the days ahead of me. My heart was so heavy that every breath was a chore. If I gave in to my tears, I was sure that even the oceans would marvel at the sight of them all. I needed a touch. I needed perspective. Where was he?

As I drove to the airport that morning, I realized that the weather was passionately displaying the same emotions bearing down on my soul. It was dark. It was dreary. It was oppressive. And as I took my seat on the plane and prepared for the long trip, I was very much aware of the hard rain pounding wildly against my window. I closed my eyes and took a deep breath, thinking it would be a miracle if I got through this day. As the plane took off, climbing higher and higher, I felt myself sinking deeper and deeper into a pool of hopelessness. I stared out the window, while my thoughts moved in and out of the shadows in my mind.

Suddenly, in just a matter of moments, the sun shone so brightly that my eyes hurt from the change of light. Up above the sea of clouds I saw a crystal blue backdrop and a mixture of pink and purple hues outlining the sky in a most perfect way. Before I could take it all in, the voice of the Lord spoke inside of my spirit. "What you see now is what I see—and how I see," the voice said in its familiar, gentle, yet strong way. "You witnessed something totally different only moments ago. Never would you have believed that right above those clouds is what looks like paradise. Peaceful. Calm. Beautiful. Whatever you see, whatever you feel, whatever is happening around you does not change the reality that I will still shine and that I am still God. I will take you through and past the storms. Things aren't what they seem. You see in such a finite way. I see eternally."

He came. He heard. He met me. I felt a weight lift as the Lord humbled my heart and drew me close. He gave me that touch, that perspective I so badly needed.

Now when I encounter the hard days, I often remember that moment on the airplane. I long to trust him more. I yearn to see as he does.

My prayer is that you and I will grow richer and deeper in our faith so that nothing in this life will cause us to despair. Our God sees beyond our circumstances and feelings to his truth, to what really does exist. Trust him.

Hiding
under
the shelter of your
wings,
I am
protected
from
the storms
that
rain upon
my life,
the heavy drops
and
slashing sleet
of
painful
memories
splattering
to the ground.
I can see them
so vividly,
collecting
together
in their little
puddles,
waiting
for someone
to splash me
with them.

Thank you, Lord,
that with
your warm
covering,
these storms aren't
able
to fall on me,
weighing me
down,
flooding my
heart,
and
drenching
my soul.
I know
I don't ever
have to fear,
for it's only
in a matter
of moments
that
they're all
dried up
by the reminder
of all you've done
and all I'm
becoming.

∞

PURE HEARTS

❧

The LORD does not look at the things man looks at. Man looks at the outward appearance, but the LORD looks at the heart.

1 Samuel 16:7

I started reading the Bible in 1978.

I'd heard scripture read during mass or at weddings and funerals throughout my childhood, but I'd never opened the Bible and explored for myself what was inside. I often joke that the Bible in my house back then was about the size of Utah and either sitting on an end table or displayed in a bedroom somewhere.

It's been many years now since I first discovered my Lord in the scriptures—his life, his words, his promises. The same yesterday, today, and forever. The Word of God is living and active. I'm often amazed at how truly alive it is. Haven't you heard people say, "I've read that verse so many times, but it hit me in a new way today"? That happens to me all the time.

I recently read 1 Corinthians 4:5, which says, "He will bring to light what is hidden in darkness and will expose the motives of men's hearts. At that time each will receive his praise from God." *God will expose the motives of our hearts.* This verse hits me at my core, and it is my core the Lord is concerned about. Most of us look pretty good on the outside. We say the "right" things, are involved in the "right" things. Our works are noble. Our lives seem to be in decent order. We may even enjoy a reputation of integrity. But the Lord looks beyond all that and deep into our hearts, and he sees exactly from what source our waters flow. Are we drinking from the river of life or from streams that originate in our own will? I pray we will all desire pure hearts and pure motives, that we will let his light pierce through the darkness in us to expose all that is not of him.

I've learned a certain prayer from a great woman of God. I pray it regularly, and I offer it to you now:

Deliver me, O Jesus,
From the desire of being loved
From the desire of being extolled
From the desire of being honored
From the desire of being praised
From the desire of being preferred
From the desire of being consulted
From the desire of being approved
From the desire of being popular
From the fear of being humiliated
From the fear of being despised
From the fear of suffering rebukes
From the fear of being calumniated
From the fear of being forgotten
From the fear of being wronged

From the fear of being ridiculed
From the fear of being suspected

Mother Teresa, *A Simple Path*

It is in the name of Jesus I pray.

Father,
   I feel like I'm truly
      beginning to learn
that without you
      everything is nothing,
   and
      with you,
   nothing
      is
         everything.

❈

LOVE ONE ANOTHER

Love must be sincere.

Romans 12:9

esus said that, because of the way we love one another, the world would know him. And Paul says that "the entire law is summed up in a single command: 'Love your neighbor as yourself'" (Galatians 5:14). This puts everything about Christianity in perspective. This is the Lord's heart for us, for his church. But I believe we desperately fall short of this command. I've traveled this country for many years, and I've met thousands of people from different denominations. Some cities seem to have a church on every corner. I often wonder if they ever join together during the course of a year. Is it possible to join together amidst the "he believes this" and "she believes that" and "of course, our way is the truth, so we take pity on the other lost souls"? If those words are not uttered aloud, I have seen actions that have definitely expressed the same mentality. If this is the way the body of Christ relates to one other, how can the true love of God flow out of our gates to reach a world in need? There are many "one anothering" verses in scripture. Here are a few:

> Love one another.
> Let us not judge one another.
> Care for one another.
> Live in peace with one another.
> Be kind to one another.
> Do not lie to one another.
> Comfort one another.
> Pray for one another.
> Give preference to one another.
> Build up one another.
> Serve one another.
> Confess your sins to one another.
> Speak to one another.
> Admonish one another.
> Encourage one another.
> Bear one another's burdens.

I am humbled when I read how God wants me to treat others, and I know I need to grow in my heart's capacity to love in a way that puts others above myself. What if you and I were videotaped for at least a week— every day, all day—at home, at work, at play—and then the video played back for our church, family, friends, anyone who looks up to us? Would we talk and act differently? Would we live differently? Does the very thought of a daily videotape send shivers up your spine? It would show so much about how we live and who we are living for. The truth is that God *is* watching. He *is* aware. Not with a gigantic teaching stick in one hand and a check-off list in the other, but with eyes that see to our very core—eyes desiring that we live in the riches of his grace so that we may be able to eat of the good fruit that comes from a life rooted in love. Now *that* is abundant life.

Let us not love from the well of our own life experiences, and through our own grids, but let us love from the well of God and own the heart he has for people. It is here that we will find an endless resource from which to give. "But if we love one another, God lives in us and his love is made complete in us" (1 John 4:12).

Take my eyes
  so
    totally
      off myself
that
    I see nothing
      before me
but
    the needs
      of others.

❦

We want to hear from you. Please send your comments about
this book to us in care of the address below. Thank you.

ZondervanPublishingHouse
Grand Rapids, Michigan 49530
http://www.zondervan.com